Firewing

David Pearson

methuen | drama

LONDON • NEW YORK • OXFORD • NEW DELHI • SYDNEY

METHUEN DRAMA
Bloomsbury Publishing Plc, 50 Bedford Square, London, WC1B 3DP, UK
Bloomsbury Publishing Inc, 1359 Broadway, New York, NY 10018, USA
Bloomsbury Publishing Ireland, 29 Earlsfort Terrace, Dublin 2, D02 AY28, Ireland

BLOOMSBURY, METHUEN DRAMA and the Methuen Drama logo are trademarks of Bloomsbury Publishing Plc.

First published in Great Britain 2026

Copyright © David Pearson, 2026

David Pearson has asserted his right under the Copyright, Designs and Patents Act, 1988, to be identified as Author of this work.

For legal purposes the Acknowledgements on p. iv constitute an extension of this copyright page.

Cover Design by Phoebe Larmour

All rights reserved. No part of this publication may be: i) reproduced or transmitted in any form, electronic or mechanical, including photocopying, recording or by means of any information storage or retrieval system without prior permission in writing from the publishers; or ii) used or reproduced in any way for the training, development or operation of artificial intelligence (AI) technologies, including generative AI technologies. The rights holders expressly reserve this publication from the text and data mining exception as per Article 4(3) of the Digital Single Market Directive (EU) 2019/790.

Bloomsbury Publishing Plc does not have any control over, or responsibility for, any third-party websites referred to or in this book. All internet addresses given in this book were correct at the time of going to press. The author and publisher regret any inconvenience caused if addresses have changed or sites have ceased to exist, but can accept no responsibility for any such changes.

No rights in incidental music or songs contained in the work are hereby granted and performance rights for any performance/presentation whatsoever must be obtained from the respective copyright owners.

All rights whatsoever in this play are strictly reserved and application for performance etc. should be made before rehearsals begin to the author via Bloomsbury Publishing, performance.permissions@bloomsbury.com. No performance may be given unless a licence has been obtained.

A catalogue record for this book is available from the British Library.

A catalog record for this book is available from the Library of Congress.

ISBN: PB: 978-1-3506-5474-7
ePDF: 978-1-3506-5475-4
eBook: 978-1-3506-5476-1

Series: Modern Plays

Typeset by Mark Heslington Ltd, Scarborough, North Yorkshire

For product safety related questions contact productsafety@bloomsbury.com.

To find out more about our authors and books visit www.bloomsbury.com and sign up for our newsletters.

Firewing was first performed at Hampstead Theatre Downstairs, London, on 17 April 2026, with the following cast:

Marcus	Charlie Beck
Tim	Gerard Horan
Director	Alice Hamilton
Designer	Good Teeth
Lighting Designer	Jamie Platt
Sound Designer	Harry Blake

Thank you to Greg Ripley-Duggan and everyone at Hampstead Theatre for bringing this play to life. I couldn't be happier that its home is a building full of welcoming, supportive and ridiculously talented people.

Huge thanks to the brilliant Alice Hamilton, who I feel very lucky to have at the helm of my debut play and whose support, encouragement, incredible insight and hard work developing Firewing mean a great deal to me.

Massive, massive thanks to the extraordinary cast, Gerard and Charlie. It's been a dream watching you both embody the characters so beautifully.

A special thank you to Rhianna, to the Stage Manager, Ella, and to James, Victoria and the wonderful design and production team whose hard work and genius creativity built the world of this play so perfectly.

Thank you to the legend Roy Williams whose generous mentorship and guidance on the Inspire programme changed the way I feel about myself as a writer. And thanks to all my fellow Inspirees: Aaron, Amy, Betty, Kate, Katie, Nancy and Naomi for being the best, most talented cohort I could imagine.

Thank you Mum and Dad for coming to see everything I've ever done. Thanks to Rosie for always believing in this play, Jai for your invaluable wise words over the years and to Andy and Josh for giving me a good excuse not to write on Sundays during the NFL season.

Thanks to Sian, Paige and the whole team at Methuen for publishing *Firewing*.

This play is dedicated to my favourite person in the world: Emma.

Thank you for everything.

Love you always x

Firewing

Characters

Tim, *early sixties*
Marcus, *early twenties*
Young Tim, *nineteen*
Tim's Dad, *late fifties*

Setting

A small hut, purposed as a nature photography hide on the edge of Dawn Lake, out in the sticks in rural South East England.

Present day / Many years ago.

Notes

The characters of **Young Tim** *and* **Tim's Dad** *should be played by the same actors who play* **Marcus** *and* **Tim** *respectively.*

Note to the reader: This text went to press before the end of rehearsals, and so may differ slightly from the show as performed.

Scene One

The Hide, on the edge of Dawn Lake.

An old wooden hut.

Along the wall, a battered old chair and desk sit below two windows; one has a camouflaged hole cut into it. An expensive – but not brand new – camera with a large, expensive lens attached is clamped onto the table, peeking through to the outside.

In the other corner, a table holding a bread bin, a kettle, a tray of mugs, an old radio and a lamp. Under the table is an old fridge and a plastic storage box, full of things.

On the back wall, two doors.

One is closed; the toilet – the door is at an angle.

The other is open; a small cubby hole room with a chair and window, overlooking the lake.

A well-worn sofa in the middle of the room.

It's mid-afternoon and the sound of birds skimming the water outside with the tips of their wings can be heard.

Occasional and slight sounds of nature.

Tim *and* **Marcus** *stand across from each other.*

Tim *is holding a wrench.*

Tim Won't be shitting, will you?

Marcus *Er . . .*

Tim Will you?

Marcus I'm –

Tim – Shitting? You won't be, will you?

Marcus Sorry, I'm –

Tim – What? You're what?

Marcus I'm Marcus.

Tim Marcus. You won't be shitting, will you? Toilet won't take it.

Marcus Should be alright, mate.

Tim Good. There's a compost heap round the back. For emergencies.

Marcus Okay . . .

Tim You're late.

Tim *enters the toilet and works at the cistern.*

Marcus *walks round the room as he speaks, investigating every corner.*

Marcus No taxis from the station, not many buses come all the way out here.

Tim *flushes the toilet. It's a very weak-sounding flush.*

Marcus Bus driver wasn't chatty, not used to seeing people much I guess, and the map they gave me is a bit confusing, so.

Marcus *stops by the camera and looks at it in detail, but doesn't touch it.*

I did text. I sent a text, saying I'd be . . .

Tim *flushes the toilet again. An even weaker flush.*

He gives up and walks into the room.

Marcus *takes in the Hide.* **Tim** *takes in* **Marcus**.

Marcus Quite remote, ain't it?

Tim I like it.

Marcus Nah, it is nice, it's really nice.

Tim No one can hear you scream out here.

Marcus Yeah. That's quite a weird thing to sa –

Tim – So.

Marcus So . . .

Tim What?

Marcus Nah, sorry. I was just, like, repeating –

Tim – Know your way round a camera?

Marcus Oh. Er, well –

Tim – Know the basics or have I got a proper Kermit?

Marcus Um. Kermit? I don't . . .

Tim Kermit. Shrek. The Incredible bloody Hulk.

Marcus Um . . .

Tim Green. Green.

Are you green, son? Or know your way round a lens?

Marcus Oh right, yeah, I mean, you've got the flash, haven't you?

And the, like, the lens, and the shutter and everything.

Tim Why are you naming parts of a camera?

Marcus Well, I'm . . . I wouldn't say I'm all that –

Tim – Enough said.

Marcus But I do like it. I enjoy it.

Tim What?

Marcus Just, taking photos and stuff.

Get it from my dad.

Yeah . . . So . . .

Happy to be here, though.

Tim This weekend we'll be going over some of the techniques I've developed over the years, and –

Marcus *laughs.*

Tim What?

Marcus That was a joke. Wasn't it?

Tim What was?

Marcus The skills you've *developed* over the years. Like a photo.

Like developing a photo.

Tim The techniques I've, *built up*, over the years.

A chance for you to experience what it's like being a professional wildlife photographer, and learn what it takes to create the work I've made across my career.

Marcus That was good. You're good at doing that bit.

Tim You've been on my website so you know who I am.

Marcus Yeah. It's a bit basic.

Tim Good.

Marcus You should get on social media.

Tim No I shouldn't. Tea?

Marcus Er, yeah, thanks.

Awkward silence for a few moments.

Marcus Do you want me to . . .?

Tim Yeah.

Marcus Right. Sorry, thought you were offering.

Tim Son.

Can you make tea, at least?

Marcus Yeah, I mean, I help out at home.

Tim Need to make a half decent cuppa if you're to stay here.

Marcus Right, yeah, um, sugar?

Tim Course.

Marcus How many?

Tim Need to lay down some ground rules.

Go over the basics.

As **Tim** *speaks,* **Marcus** *fiddles with the kettle and looks for a socket on the wall.*

Tim There's a lot to learn over the weekend, so you gotta muddle through, find a way to take it in. Your application showed potential, and you were chosen off the back of that, but it's very important, and I really can't be stressing this enough, that you . . .

Tim *watches* **Marcus** *struggle to reach the cable to the socket.*

Tim You listening?

Marcus Oh, yeah, I'm just, is there . . .?

Tim You gonna fill it?

Marcus Empty, yeah, course it is.

Tim Well, I tend to make my tea with, you know, liquid.

And then I drink it. And then it's gone.

So yeah, course it's empty, you wally.

Now, are you listening to me?

Stop, just stop and listen. The matter with you?

Marcus Do you want me to make a tea, mate, or stop and listen?

Tim Please, God, I haven't got someone worse than the last kid.

Marcus I'm just saying I can't –

Tim – Hundreds of entries there were, and have mercy if I've picked someone who finds a kettle too high tech. Need to be able to do a few things at once.

Made tea before, I'm guessing?

Marcus I'm twenty-two.

Tim Son, when you're as daft as you seem to be, *never* tell people your real age. Makes you seem thick as a plank.

Marcus I'm not.

Tim Thick as a fucking thick plank.

Marcus I'm not thick, mate.

Tim First step's the manual. Did they send you it?

Marcus Manual? Nah.

Tim Useless, that lot.

I said if he's gonna be greener than The Grinch, you'd better at least give him the manual.

Marcus Just gave me a time, a place, said to come here, you know, to get going.

Tim Get going? Did they say '*get going*'?

Tim *searches the storage box for something.*

Marcus What's in it, the, er, the manual?

Tim Instructions. Rules. You'll wanna follow them. Closely.

Marcus What was wrong with him, the last guy?

Tim Don't worry about the last fella, he's not worrying about you. But I'd have wrapped that cord round his throat if he tried to boil an empty kettle, know that.

I'll put it down to first day nerves, for pity on you.

And you can thank me for it.

Marcus Yeah.

Cheers, mate.

Tim How are you with boring?

Cos it can get boring in here for some people.

Marcus Yeah. I can believe that.

Tim If you find it boring, this ain't for you.

Marcus Thought you'd have your awards up and all that.

You've done, you know, like, some quite good stuff.

Tim *'Some quite good stuff.'*

Tim *pulls a large red laminated manual from the box and throws it to* **Marcus**.

Marcus I have to read all this?

Tim Get familiar with it.

Marcus Today?

Tim Most important bits at the front.

Marcus Right.

Tim Front sixty, seventy pages.

Marcus Right. Great . . .

Tim You gotta do this properly, starts with that.

Read the first chapter, we can move on.

Tim *sits at the camera and cleans it with a cloth.*

Marcus *wanders round, holding the manual but not really reading it.*

A bird flies past the window.

Marcus Whoa.

See that?

Tim What?

Marcus Massive fucking peacock-looking thing just flew past. Just right by the window, flew past, just then.

Marcus *stares out of the window.*

After a moment he returns to the kettle and pours two teas.

Sugar?

Tim Two.

Marcus Did you build this place?

Tim No.

They drink their tea.

The fish eagle.

Marcus Oh, yeah.

Yeah?

Tim It's a good photograph.

Marcus Oh, cheers.

Tim On holiday, your application said.

Marcus Yeah, I was just sat there, on the seafront with my old man, he's clued up on all that, nature and birds and stuff, and he pointed it out, just up at the sky and said, *'Get the camera'*, so I did, you know.

Didn't know it was rare 'til after, when I went and looked it up. But I'm alright with a camera.

Tim *'Nature and birds and stuff.'*

Photographer, is he?

Marcus Who?

Tim Old man, he a photographer, then?

Marcus Yeah, well, not professional or anything, but he loves it. Takes his camera everywhere, house was always full of equipment.

Tim His camera, was it?

Marcus Nah, mine.

He gave me it. It was only basic.

Tim And it took that?

Marcus Yeah.

Tim Lucky to get lighting like that with no prep and basic kit.

Marcus I guess . . .

What about your Dad, did he take photos?

Tim No. No, he didn't.

Marcus Okay.

Beat.

Tim *looks through the camera and snaps a photograph.*

Marcus What was that?

Tim That, you dopey sod, was a photograph.

Marcus Of what?

Tim *'Of what?'*

'Of what?'

Marcus Yeah, what was the photo of?

Marcus *stands over* **Tim**, *getting very close.*

Tim Right. Okay. The rules.

Tim *points* **Marcus** *to the sofa. They sit across from each other.*

Tim I'll keep this basic, okay? So even you can follow.

Marcus Yeah. Er, thanks.

Tim This is the camera.

Marcus Thought it was, yeah.

Tim My camera.

Marcus Yeah.

Tim And you don't touch it.

Marcus Okay.

Tim That's rule number one. The most important rule. It's rule number one, number two and number three. You. Don't. Touch it.

And if you break that rule, you're straight out on your ear, okay? You get that don't you?

Marcus Yes.

Tim So don't touch it.

Marcus Cool.

Tim No. No, it's not cool.

Marcus Yeah, no, I just meant –

Tim – Just leave it, Marcus, it's simple.

Marcus Leave it. Got it. Yeah.

Beat.

But we might use it, maybe, tomorrow?

Tim Marcus, why are you here?

Marcus Got invited.

Tim Because?

Marcus Cos I applied. To take pictures and stuff. For you to teach me.

Least that's what I thought.

Tim You planned on just turning up and snapping some lovely birds?

Marcus No.

Beat.

Well yeah, alright, yeah I did kind of think that a bit, mate. Just . . . you didn't get all your exhibitions, your awards, didn't get all that by sitting reading, did you? Thought I'd learn properly, that's why I entered.

Tim You will learn, by watching me, by doing everything I tell you to do.

Marcus Don't seem the best use of time, does it, sat on my arse reading a guidebook.

Tim Manual.

Marcus But you know all of it, by heart?

Tim I wrote it, so yeah, I do.

Marcus So someone taught you though, yeah?

Tim They did '*though, yeah*'.

Marcus I won't be taking any photos today, then?

Tim Oh, you might.

I mean you can, I won't stop you. You can get your phone out and snap away.

Snap, cute little photo of a duckie. Aw.

Snap, beautifully framed selfie of you in the cubby.

Bet you've already sent your parents a picture of the lake, ain't you?

Hmm.

Photos.

They're not *photographs*, Marcus.

Marcus Thought we'd be out there.

Tim Have you ever learnt anything?

Anything of use?

Anything you had to stick with, master, dedicate yourself to?

Anything at all like that, Marcus?

Marcus I can cook a bit. Taught myself.

Tim Right.

Well, then. Listen.

Stop trying to skip steps and just listen.

You don't grab a camera and snap away at everything you see.

You don't, you just don't.

This just something you do with your old man, is it? Cos that's fine, that's great, but that's not what this is, you know that, don't you?

Isn't a hobby. And you have to learn properly, take it serious.

Tim *points at the manual.*

Just the first bit. Sooner you read it sooner we can move on.

Marcus I bet you never had a proper job, an actual, put your back out every day, get home late, get up early and do it all again the next day type job, have you?

We all take photos, mate.

Tim Yeah.

But some of us are actually fucking good at it.

'Mate.'

Marcus *lies down on the sofa, begins reading the manual.*

Tim *sits carefully and looks out through the camera at the lake.*

Silence for a while.

Marcus You really don't ever get bored? Honestly, in a place like thi –

Tim – My first lens was only a little Canon.

Had a cheap camera but this lens was half decent. Didn't know what to do with it really. Fiddled about, managed to get it on the camera eventually.

Couldn't believe it, I . . .

Yeah.

Couldn't believe it.

Made everything suddenly, somehow, more . . . alive. Like I could really see what I was looking at, nothing between me and the picture, you know?

My old teacher used to say, '*A good lens feels like it isn't there*'. and I finally, actually knew what he meant.

I don't get bored, no.

Not after you've seen it like that, out there.

Silence for a moment.

Tim *takes a photograph.*

Scene Two

The Hide.

Early evening.

A Kodak Carousel projector is set up in the middle of the Hide, loaded up with slides.

It is angled at the wall and **Tim** *is projecting some of his wildlife photography onto it.*

Tim *and* **Marcus** *sit and watch in silence as half a dozen stunning photographs of different animals flash up in front of them.*

Marcus Nah, to be fair . . .

Beat.

To be fair, they are fucking good.

Tim *flicks through the photographs at a faster pace.*

Marcus Hold on.

Nah, hold on, what was that one?

Tim *skips through the photographs then stops on one.*

A beautifully shot photograph of an eagle gliding in mid-air, wings outstretched and sharp beak pointing down.

Tim You see?

Marcus Yeah.

Beat.

See what?

Tim The similarity.

Marcus Between?

Tim This one and yours, the fish eagle.

Marcus Well . . .

Tim Go on.

Marcus Well, they're both birds, aren't they?

Both birds in the air.

Tim Look at it.

Marcus Yeah . . .

Tim They're similar.

Marcus They're not.

Tim Need to look at it properly.

Marcus Did you take that?

Tim Reminded me of this when I saw it. Could be that good, yours, I'm telling you, son. Few tweaks, but you've got the basics down.

I can help with that, make them better, all of your photographs.

Don't that excite you? You might be a thick lad, but I can –

Marcus – I'm not thick –

Tim – Get you documenting the world, right? Telling stories through your photographs. Yours was good, so I'm just saying you . . .

I think you've got something.

Why I chose you.

Marcus Was it really the only reason, the photo?

Tim I'm saying this cos I . . .

Look, I'm like a cat.

Marcus Are you?

Tim If I don't like you, you'd never see me.

But, for some reason, and it's completely beyond me why, but I . . .

You've got a, a chance, I think. Is all I'm saying.

Marcus I wouldn't say you give off cat vibes.

Tim Yeah? Well, I might scratch both your fucking eyes out.

Marcus Cool.

Well, no, not cool, but . . .

Tim Tell me again.

Marcus Tell you what?

Tim About when you took it, the story.

Marcus . . . I just took it.

Tim Come on, Marcus.

Marcus I took it. I just took it.

Tim See. You don't just take a photograph, don't just take it.

You form it, you light it, you frame it, you mould it. You, you . . .

Create it.

You create it.

Marcus Well shit, I didn't.

I just took it.

Marcus *flicks through the photographs.*

He stops on a picture of a fox waiting to pounce on a rabbit. It's a beautifully lit, bright photograph with glinting blades of grass across a vast, sunny field.

You love animals, don't you?

Tim Do I?

Marcus You spend your life looking at them.

Tim And?

Marcus Well, this rabbit, then. About to be eaten –

Tim – Oh, okay –

Marcus – torn to shreds by the fox –

Tim – *This?* We're doing *this?* –

Marcus – And you're sat watching, how can you say you love animals?

Don't make sense.

Tim It's observing.

Marcus It's cruel.

Tim Cruel to observe nature?

Marcus For showing something cruel, and not stepping in.

Tim And doing what?

Marcus Alright, so there's this picture I saw of a woman from Indonesia or somewhere, and she's being punished for adultery, right, they've stuck her in a box, locked it up and they're letting her starve, out in the desert.

Tim Yeah, I know it.

Marcus She's reaching out trying to undo the lock.

Tim It's Mongolia.

Marcus Someone stood there, watching that, her reaching for her life, literally for her life, mate, and they did nothing, just took the picture.

Tim And now we've a document of it, what people were put through.

Even someone like you, with very few brain cells bouncing around your skull know about it when you wouldn't have.

Marcus She was starving to death, mate.

Not an animal, an actual person.

Tim Will have haunted the photographer their whole life, poor bastard.

Marcus So he was right, then, to do nothing, let her die in the box?

Tim Don't matter about right or wrong, it's –

Marcus – I'm asking, if they were right to do that, or should they have helped her?

Tim It's important to see how things are, how they actually are.

Marcus I couldn't do that, man.

Tim He steps in, he's disturbing the truth, that's not his job.

Marcus It's not right.

Tim You're observing. You're recording, capturing nature, life, the world. As it is.

Not how you want to see it.

Marcus, son, you are not God.

Marcus *stares at the photograph.*

Tim You sure this is for you?

Marcus I think I just . . . my dad was good at it, and Mum, like, paints, sometimes, like she's a really good painter. Even if the view from the flat's shite.

So I've always wondered if this kind of thing is, sort of, in my blood a bit.

Tim *watches* **Marcus** *for a few moments.*

Tim . . . Position of the camera takes us to ground level. You see?

We feel involved in the action, from the rabbit's point of view, poor sod. Helps frame the background and all; a wilderness, a massive plain of life. Action, drama, real drama, a great big land of possibility.

You see that?

Beat.

Marcus Like it's, I dunno, the, the centre of the world, but don't really matter? Like in the grand scheme?

Tim *is happy with the answer but doesn't allow himself to show it.*

Marcus Yeah. I sort of get that.

Tim Contrast between the beautiful open-ended scenery and the pure horror about to happen right in front of the lens, front and centre, that's captivating, that's . . .

That's a fucking photograph.

Marcus *continues to stare at the photograph for a moment.*

Marcus Contrast and all that? That's . . .

Yeah, a lot to take in, innit?

Bloody good though, to be fair to you, mate.

Did it survive?

Tim Picked someone who knows fuck all about animals.

Marcus The rabbit, did it make it?

Tim Knows absolutely fuck all about cameras, and even less about animals.

Marcus A little bit, I know a little bit, just have to train my eyes, don't I?

Tim That means, what, you need glasses?

Marcus Twenty-twenty vision, me.

Tim It was torn to shreds, the rabbit, course it was. And no, I didn't take a photograph of that cos I'm not psychotic. If that bothers you, you'll wanna get out more. Stuck inside, that'll drive you mad, scared to look out the window in case you see a rabbit decapitated.

Mind you, maybe best you stay indoors, do yourself and everyone else a right damage out there, daft as a brush with your untrained eyes.

Marcus Eyes work fine.

Marcus *groans, lies back on the sofa.*

See this place clear enough.

Thought it'd be. I dunno.

Tim Thought what?

Marcus Get an idea of a place in your head, don't you? Then you go somewhere and it's, well, not that.

Tim Got everything I need.

Marcus *looks round at the room.*

Marcus Where we sleeping then?

Tim I'm on the sofa bed. There's an air mattress you can lay out in the cubby.

Marcus Got a pump for it?

Tim Yeah, but the air goes in one end and straight out the puncture, so I wouldn't bother.

Marcus *looks up at the walls.*

Marcus It's a bit, sort of, rustic, didn't think it'd be so . . . wooden.

Tim Give it a rest.

Marcus There's a tiny little park round where I live. Used to have all sorts, plants from all over the world, they kept it all nice and colourful, flowerbeds full of stuff. Council closed it down, overgrown now, you can't even get in there.

Could be nice, really nice, always think about that when I walk past, about how nice it could be.

It's a bit like that in here.

Tim So, what, a dump?

Marcus Nah, not a dump, I'm saying it's –

Tim – Does the job.

Marcus Yeah, I know.

Tim Does what I need it to.

Marcus Could, like, liven it up a bit maybe.

Tim No.

Marcus Seen nicer hospital wards.

Tim Don't be a prick.

Marcus Seen nicer prison cells.

Tim What?

You haven't, have you? Been inside?

Marcus You're like that woman, that Indonesian woman.

Tim Mongolian.

Marcus Trapped, locked in a box, that's your life, but you chose it, that's the only difference between you and her.

Tim Wasn't on the info they gave me.

Tim *pulls a sheet of paper from his pocket and closely scrutinises it.*

Marcus I mean, how many days do you reckon, across your whole life, you've spent sat inside this box, like, cut off from the world?

Tim Didn't put it on here, if you've got a criminal record.

Marcus '*Documenting*' the world but not living in it.

Tim Says about school, a few issues at school but nothing about prison, youth offenders.

Marcus What does it say about school?

Tim You been to prison, son?

Marcus What if I have? Is that it, we done?

Tim Had problems before, people came here and they . . .

It's not an issue, it ain't, but if you've lied, then it becomes an issue.

Marcus Well I haven't.

Tim *puts down the paper,* **Marcus** *picks it up and reads it.*

Tim I've had . . . disputes, before, problems with some kids.

Marcus Yeah, you said. Who gave you this?

Tim Don't matter to me if someone's been inside.

Marcus Yeah, you seem fine with it, mate.

Tim No, I'm not saying –

Marcus – Visited.

That's it. That's all.

Tim They weren't bad kids or nothing, thought it'd work but it got . . . difficult, and they weren't honest.

Marcus Mate, who gave you this?

Tim It's the lying that don't sit right with me. And they didn't take it seriously, didn't wanna try, but it's not cos they'd been to prison, not wrong 'uns, I wouldn't write them off like that.

Marcus Who did you speak to about me, Tim? My old school?

Tim *sits and flicks through some more photographs.*

They both watch them in silence for a few moments.

Tim I wouldn't write them off like everyone else, just cos . . .

But I need someone to help.

And I, for a second I worried you lied to me.

I need someone to help. That's all.

Tim *walks over and flicks the kettle on.*

Marcus Tim?

Tim '*A few issues*', they said.

But that you're a good kid.

Marcus Yeah. Well. '*Issues.*'

They don't help me, never have, so they can do one.

Silence for a moment as the kettle boils.

Think I've got a migraine coming on.

Tim *opens a tin of beans and drinks straight from it.*

Marcus Mate, don't. You'll make me sick.

Tim Limited options for dinner, I'm afraid.

I've noodles, some fish, load of tins. If your favourite food comes in tins, you're a lucky boy.

Marcus Not hungry.

Tim More tins than Andy Warhol.

He waits. Nothing.

Probably won't get that, will you?

Nothing.

Oi.

I said I doubt you'd get that, do you? Even know who Warhol is, son?

Marcus Are you talking to me?

Tim Fuck me, I'm trying to.

Marcus Difficult to tell sometimes.

Tim You taking the piss?

Marcus Nah, I just mean someti –

Tim – Gonna have a right laugh, ain't we, me and you?

Tim *finishes the beans.*

Marcus *flicks through the manual.*

Marcus . . . Got anything nice for the morning? For breakfast?

Tim Don't eat it.

Marcus What? That's nuts.

Tim Don't eat it. Never have.

You'll survive a couple of nights.

Marcus You want a bit of bacon, eggs benedict or something.

Tim No I don't.

Marcus It's good, gets you going, it's the –

Tim – I swear to God, Marcus, if you're about to say it's the most important meal of the day.

Marcus *was about to, but he doesn't.*

Tim Don't be so, unoriginal.

Eggs benedict? Who the fuck do you think you are?

If you're gonna get all gourmet about it you can have the beans with the sausages in.

Marcus I'm alright for now, mate.

Tim You gotta have something to keep you going. Gonna be a long night, long couple of days.

Tim *makes a tea.*

Marcus Got a flannel?

Beat.

Said you got a flannel?

Tim You make a lot of noise. Make less noise.

Marcus I'm burning up.

Tim Said in the email. Have to bring your own medicine if you need it.

Swear I'd better not catch it, Marcus.

Marcus It's a migraine. I said.

Tim I mean it, you'd better not give me it. Not come down with anything in ages, not starting now.

Marcus Can't catch migraines. Unless you inherit it. Another thing she's passed down to me, cheers, Mum.

What's the secret, then, to never getting ill?

Tim Fresh air.

Not the same set of walls all day every day.

Marcus Suppose you need human contact to catch something.

Tim God, you are hilarious.

Marcus Does you all sorts of good, then, being outside.

So let's go out and just take some –

Tim – No.

Marcus I pick things up really quickly.

Tim *points at the camera.*

Tim (*shouts*) Well you don't pick *that* up!

Hear me?

Awkward silence for a moment.

Marcus *rolls onto his back, groans.*

Tim You can stop that, and all.

Marcus Got a temperature.

Tim About the second worst person they've ever sent.

Marcus This other guy, must've done something really bad.

Tim He never even made it to the manual. Count yourself lucky.

Marcus Yeah. I'm truly blessed.

Tim . . . Is it someone from your family, then? Who's inside?

Marcus Oh . . . nah . . . friend. Old friend.

From school.

Tim How long did he get?

Marcus Long.

Tim What'd he do?

Marcus It's just . . . he was fine, he was alright, he . . . had some bad luck, things happened to him.

Tim What things?

Marcus He was, well, he lives in the middle of nowhere, right, and he was out on this hill one night, on his way home, and he saw these cars down in this, like, this valley.

Tim Right . . .

Marcus Goes down there and all the cars are empty, but they've been shot up and everything, really bad scene, type of thing we'd avoid, me and you, you know, cos we know better. But he's a bit . . .

And there's a couple of bodies and someone's killed a dog and it's just carnage, chaos.

Tim I think I . . .

Marcus What?

Tim No, go on.

Marcus What?

Tim Nah, it's just . . . might've seen it, on the news maybe, rings a . . . go on . . .

Marcus There's this fella in one of the cars and he's, like, really on death's door, begging for water.

My mate, though, he finds this bag of money and takes off with it.

But he gets home and starts regretting leaving the guy to bleed out, so he makes a big mistake, he goes back.

And he's back down in the valley, right, giving the guy water, and these men come flying down after him with guns and all sorts and their dog starts chasing him so he has to run across this little river, and when he gets –

Tim – That's *No Country for Old Men.*

Marcus . . . It is, yeah.

Tim *finishes his tea.*

Marcus *groans.*

Marcus I'm gonna get the shits, I know it, always do when I get a bug. Can't win with these things.

Come and feel it, my head.

Have you got a flannel or something? Ice?

Tim No.

Marcus Sorry, mate, not a shop or anything round here, is there?

Tim Ten mins up the road if you're quick.

Shuts in fifteen.

Marcus Ugh.

Can't sit up, how am I gonna get to a shop?

Tim (*in Scottish accent*) Have to ride it out, then, won't ya, Renton?

Cold turkey.

Nothing. Again.

Tim *Trainspotting* . . .

Marcus Are all of your references from, like, fifty years ago?

Tim You got a migraine and a dodgy tummy?

Marcus The whole lot.

Whole shebang.

Marcus *tries to stand, groans and lies back down.*

Tim Ride it out.

In silence, and all.

Marcus So I gotta get over it really quick and completely quiet.

Tim The size of it, yeah.

Marcus I'm using the toilet.

Tim Are you fuck.

Marcus Where else am I supposed to go? Kind of place have I come to?

Tim I told you when you got here –

Marcus – And I'm telling you I ain't squatting over a bush all night.

I'm gonna have to leave, can't sit like this all weekend.

Marcus *struggles to get up.* **Tim** *watches him for a moment.*

Marcus You got a number for a taxi, mate? Better go.

Tim Go?

Marcus Feeling rough. Need to get home, sleep it off.

Sorry. You can, I dunno, get someone else in to make the tea, can't you?

Beat.

Tim I can't just . . .

Right.

So I'm going to the shop?

Marcus I mean, if you don't mind.

Tim You understand rule one, don't you?

Marcus Oh, for f . . .

Tim Marcus.

Don't you?

Marcus I'm ill, man!

Tim You break that rule, you're gone.

Clear?

Marcus Yes.

Tim *puts on his coat.*

Tim So don't touch it.

And that doesn't mean you can stroke it, lift it, change the angle, even look at it, cos that counts as breaking the rule. And I'll know.

Marcus Yeah.

Probably have a quick nap. Power nap.

Tim Paracetamol and water, what else?

Marcus Kit Kat?

Tim Fuck off.

Marcus Right.

Tim Be back in a bit.

Tim *hovers for a moment.*

Just stay there.

Don't touch it.

Tim *exits.*

After a moment, **Marcus** *shoots up from the sofa and looks out of the window.*

He pulls out his phone but can't get a signal.

He moves around the cabin, lifting his phone in the air.

He settles in the cubby hole – the only place he can get a signal – and dials.

Marcus (*into the phone*) Yeah. Alright?

Yeah, yeah, I'm here.

Here, I'm here, mate, the photographer.

Marcus *goes to the camera.*

Where do I find that?

Marcus *very carefully lifts the camera to look underneath.*

Oh. Serial.

Z24489378.

378.

Losing signal, he returns to the cubby hole.

No, 3 . . . 7 . . . 8 . . .

Alright. And you can scratch that, yeah?

Okay, cool.

Yeah, and I can do two lenses as well.

Yeah. Yeah, they're big.

Sort it with them now, yeah?

Let me know.

Then I can leave.

Make sure you do.

Please.

Marcus *hangs up.*

He stares at the camera.

Scene Three

The Hide.

Early evening.

Marcus *reads the manual.*

Tim *bursts through the door holding a carrier bag,* **Marcus** *jumps.*

Tim He's a tight-fisted old sod.

Marcus Tim, mate, don't come through the door like that.

Tim It's the only shop for miles.

Marcus Not when my belly's all wobbly.

Tim Puts the prices up every week. Three quid for a tiny pack of digestives. Three quid? What are they, gold plated?

Marcus They are nice though, did you get some? Used to have the chocolate ones sometimes, as a treat, cos you can dunk them in –

Tim – The story.

In full.

Put that down.

The fish eagle story.

But properly, tell me properly.

Tim *stands, waits.*

Marcus Dunno, just, on the beach with my dad, eating, and he pointed –

Tim – Eating what?

Marcus Fish and chips.

Tim *sits in his chair, settles in.*

Marcus Did you get the water?

Tim *throws* **Marcus** *the bag.*

Marcus *gulps down the water and takes some tablets from the pack.*

Tim *leans back, shuts his eyes.*

Marcus You alright, mate?

Tim Fish and chips. Sauce?

Marcus Curry.

Marcus *pockets the tablets; doesn't take any.*

Tim Good lad.

So, you're on the seafront eating fish and chips with curry sauce, sat on, what, a bench?

Marcus One of the little benches, yeah, like, looking out at sea, and he points –

Tim – Busy? Busy day on the beach?

Marcus Kind of, yeah.

Yeah, it was actually.

Remember how busy it was, more than normal.

Mum went round the shops, Dad and me were eating, using those shite wooden forks that always break.

Marcus *leans back and shuts his eyes.*

We were sat, eating, seats were kind of cold, even for a nice day. Could taste the salt from the sea when the wind came at you.

We just watched. Beach covered with people, walking along the front, running in and out the water.

Dad took all the tickets we'd won in the arcades out his bag, started counting them.

I used to fiddle with the camera he gave me every time we went out, make him think I actually use it, you know, cos it was nice of him to get me it, but I never used it much when he weren't there. Always asked if I'd got many good photos lately and I'd always just say yeah.

Really though I could never get the hang of the fucking thing and everything came out grainy.

But I'd never tell him that.

Tim *opens his eyes and watches* **Marcus** *as he speaks.*

Marcus It was just, like . . .

Weird.

It was weird.

Just when he asked about the camera all these people on the beach started pointing up. Never realise these things until you do, you know, like, how many people can spot a rare bird.

They were all pointing and Dad was fiddling about with the camera, doing all sorts so I just grabbed it and aimed up at this massive bird flying over the beach and I . . . I just took it.

He was happy.

Me, I was more worried about the arcade tickets blowing into the sea.

Marcus *opens his eyes.*

Tim And that was, what, ten years ago? Taken many since?

Marcus Yeah, like, a few. That's the best one though.

I can send the others over sometime, if you want.

Tim What lens?

Marcus Only cheap. But it was big. Big, thick, round one.

Tim *'Big, thick, round one,'* don't deafen me with jargon.

It's mad you couldn't ever get a good 'un out of the camera, but you managed to take that on it.

Marcus Suppose.

Beat.

Tim Just happens sometimes, don't it? Just happens and you have to just catch it.

Just catch it when it's in front of you.

Else it'll be gone.

Marcus Guess, yeah.

Tim *nods, considers for a moment.*

He goes to his box and pulls out more slides.

Marcus Get me a Kit Kat?

Tim You weren't hungry a minute ago.

Marcus Just don't fancy drinking a tin of beans, that's all.

Tim *loads the slides into the projector and projects onto the wall.*

A moonlit photograph of a fox, walking off into the distance on railway tracks.

The tracks are central and, in the background, a modern city and its lights illuminate the sky. The fox's crisp brown fur glistens and flows with its movement away from the camera.

They both stare at it for a moment.

Tim Just to warn you, if your answer is *'a fox'*, I'll skin you alive.

So, Marcus, what do you see?

Beat.

Marcus . . . Is it not a fox, then? Does look like one.

Tim So that's what you think when you look at this? You think, *'There's a photograph of a fox'*, and that's it?

Marcus It'll sound stupid.

Tim Goes without saying.

Marcus The tracks.

Something to do with the tracks.

Tim *is impressed, proud.*

He pulls a laser pen from his pocket.

Marcus Don't see them much these days.

Tim *points the laser at the top right corner of the photograph; a large city building.*

Tim Look here.

Marcus Right.

Beat.

Yeah?

Tim Eyes wanna move, don't they?

Marcus Yeah, sort of.

Tim To here?

Tim *points to the bottom left corner of the photograph; rubble near the train tracks.*

Marcus Nah. Nah not really.

Tim Well, keep looking there . . .

Don't feel right, does it?

Marcus Just kind of, wanna look at, like, the tracks. And the fox, I guess.

Tim Good. We're naturally drawn to lines in photographs, so you have to use them to guide people's eyes. It was really important to wait until the fox was on the actual tracks, to give you a sense of its journey, and they lead your eyes right to him, straight away.

Tim *points to the grass and debris around the train tracks in the bottom of the picture.*

Negative space.

You wanna use these areas to create breathing room for your subject, the fox in this photograph. Not always just close ups.

Not having anything too striking in the corners and edges, just grass and debris there, creates that space, the dull colours do and all, you don't want other colours screaming for attention, distracting from your subject. You see?

City in the background is contrast, the modern world at the end of the line coming all the way from nature. All helps create emotions in the viewer, why's the fox heading there, away from what we think is its habitat? Make your photographs as interesting as you can, get people to really look, take time with it, feel it.

Think. If you can get them to think, then you're . . .

You're there.

But you're in control, *you're* telling the viewer what they're seeing, what to concentrate on. Use the lines, the symmetry either side of the tracks, control how you position the subject, that's all really important.

Control where they look.

Marcus Why's it walking to the city?

Tim Exactly.

Marcus Nah, why is it walking to the city?

Tim Photography ain't about answers, Marcus.

Marcus You said it needed to be on the tracks.

Tim Yeah.

Marcus So you waited there round by the –

Tim – Four hours, I waited.

Marcus Right. Damn.

Tim In the muck, and the rain. In the dirt.

You'll need to build that up, your patience.

And your endurance, how long you can lie there still, or you'll miss it, and you won't even know you've missed it.

Marcus Yeah. Maybe not for me, then.

Tim You'll get there.

Marcus *looks at* **Tim**, *who doesn't hold his gaze.*

Marcus *can't help but smile.*

They stare at the photograph.

Tim If they're culled, they breed more, they're hard wired to live.

But cars kill a hundred thousand every year.

Silence for a moment.

Marcus Oh.

Beat.

Yeah. That makes sense actually, cos this one's, like, on the . . .

Should call it '*Survival*'.

Do you name photos? You should.

Tim This type of photography, it's the fragile beauty of the planet and life, capturing a split second of millions of years of evolution, a moment that'll never ever happen again.

Marcus Yeah, it's like, I saw a picture of a fox on the London Underground once, just sat on a train. And it took the escalator up after.

Tim Just when I think . . .

Then you're off on one about a fox riding the fucking Jubilee Line.

Marcus . . . Just when you think what?

Marcus *studies the photograph some more.*

Tim *rummages through the box and pulls out a roll of white masking tape.*

Tim Rule of thirds, heard of it?

Tim *drags the table across to the wall and stands on it.*

Over the projected image, he lays two horizontal and two vertical strips of tape, dividing the photograph into nine equal squares.

The horizon, it's on the top line.

And the tracks sit in the middle, so each side is symmetrical.

Divide your photograph into threes. Horizontal and vertical.

Marcus Ah yeah, I can get them lines up on my phone, and there's a dot you can move around to get the best photo.

Tim Don't start. You'll give *me* a migraine.

Tim *climbs down and flicks forward to the next slide.;*

A darkly lit photograph of a woodlands at night; the trees in the distance are blurred into shapes of black and the plain of grass in the foreground is a dark green.

Sitting perfectly on the intersection of the 'rule of thirds' lines in the bottom corner is a robin, sat close to the camera with a small twig in its mouth, staring out at the woodlands. Its red breast is in full colour, in contrast with the rest of the setting.

One of my favourite photographs I ever took.

Marcus . . . This one?

Tim Just look at it.

Marcus I am.

Tim Look at it.

Marcus . . . I am.

Tim In silence.

Just look.

They stare at the photograph for a while.

Marcus . . . I like the –

Tim – One step away from letting the machine take the photograph. The grid, the dot, all that on your phone. Might show the best angle, change the lighting for you, but then what? What are you looking at?

That's the most important thing. You seeing what I'm . . . what I'm seeing. That's your great weapon, Marcus. Show them what you see.

Taking the photograph's half the story, don't give that away.

Don't need endless bloody gubbins to guide your eyes and all that. When you can't do that stuff for yourself, it's time to stop.

They stare for a bit longer.

Know it's just a robin, I know that, see them everywhere. Why I never published or displayed it, but it's one of my favourites, really is.

It just . . .

Marcus *watches* **Tim** *stare at the photograph.*

Tim They're solitary bir –

Marcus – Solitary birds, yeah, I was gonna say.

Dad told me that.

Tim Took this about three-thirty in the morning.

Marcus Damn. Another all-nighter, yeah?

Tim He's there, just him, waiting for the day, waiting to face it.

On his own.

A moment.

Marcus . . . See what you mean, about the lines.

Tim The lines. Yeah.

Subject's right where it should be, see? Called power points there, where the lines meet. Put anything of interest in the power points if you can.

Horizon's on the top line again, and all.

Marcus *is really taking it in now.*

Tim That time of morning naturally gives you the low light, pulls focus away from all the colours; green grass, woodlands, trees, all blend into a dark mixture of green, grey and blue, see? He's waiting for the morning light, so are we.

Made sure the background's blurred, blocking everything else out to pull focus on him, helps he has that red breast, and I've left that for full effect.

All to control the viewer's eyes, you see?

Tell a story. Or hint at one at least.

And his positioning's important, right in front of the camera, back to us, looking out. A sense of the large world just beyond him that he's heading into for the day.

It's just him, and the world.

It's a story. Tell a story.

Silence for a moment.

Tim *'Courage'*, I called it.

I do name them.

Marcus . . . I could definitely, you know, I could see myself doing this, creating stuff like that, well, trying to, like, eventually.

Tim Yeah?

Marcus Yeah, I could see me doing it.

Get a name for myself, go round the globe, sat in ditches, seeing the world's birds.

Tim . . . South Bridge, says on your form.

Live just behind the station, right, in the estate?

Marcus . . . I do, yeah.

Tim By The Cricketers?

Marcus Yeah.

Tim In there much?

Marcus Nah, but it's nice to have somewhere to go if I'm at a loose end and bored of having all my organs in one piece.

You know The Cricketers?

Tim Played darts there when I was a nipper.

Won so much they used to chase me out. Don't think I ever lost in that pub.

Still the bookies next door?

Marcus The bookies, yeah. Loads of them.

Tim Old man spent a lot of time in there.

Marcus You from South Bridge?

Tim Yeah. Parents moved there when I was little.

Always been the same, hardly any good schools.

Wrote off all my mates. Got told they'd mess up their lives.

So they did.

Marcus Sounds about right.

Tim Had this teacher, only one who, well . . .

Ran a photography club after school, only me turned up. He got sick of it round there in the end, pissed off to Australia.

Tim *walks to his box and pulls out a small metal tin.*

He opens it; inside is just one slide.

He removes the other slides from the projector, carefully places them back in their box.

He loads the single slide.

A grainy, blurred, low resolution picture of a large, beautiful, majestic bird high over a small lake.

It has a bright, golden chest and a black and white spotted beak.

Its wings are a fiery red.

Marcus . . . That's a shit one.

Tim Firewing.

Only time it's ever been seen in this country.

Marcus Your camera skills have shot up at least.

They stare at the photograph.

Beat.

Never seen anything like it.

Tim Won't have done.

It's reclusive.

Marcus Yeah?

Tim From Siberia. Only came over here once, not sure why, maybe a brutal winter, maybe got lost migrating, caught in the wind, ended up flying across the North Sea and inland to here, perfect for them really, these woodlands.

Beat.

They say it's a fake.

Marcus Who?

Tim Everyone. All of them. They think it's a lie, that I lied.

Marcus Why?

Tim They're out there, aren't they, every month of the year on a hillside on the east coast, all tucked under their coats and their brollies, stood up on a cliff for ten, twelve hours, huddled together in the pissing rain, all the experts with their calendars and their predictions and their calculations of migration routes, waiting to spot a rare bird or a new species so they can jot it down in their little notebooks.

So they can't bear it, can they? That they've never seen it but he came here, to me.

Marcus Why don't they go there, then?

Tim What?

Marcus To see it, why don't they go to Siberia?

Tim Siberia's big, really big.

Can't just turn up there with binoculars and expect to bump into it. Only been spotted a handful of times and not for years and years. They reckon it might even be extinct.

Marcus Yeah?

Tim But it isn't.

Marcus Right. Okay.

Tim What?

Marcus Well.

You know that, do you? You seem really sure, that's all.

Tim I am sure.

Marcus If there's that many people and they're all saying it.

Tim I'm sure.

They say it's, I dunno, a buzzard or an eagle or a bloody great big flying chicken and I've coloured its wings red, faked it.

They stopped putting on my exhibitions for a bit, tried to embarrass me. Caused me no end of grief.

Marcus Yeah, it's like, this kid at school, Niall, kept getting the shit kicked out of him, so he went round telling everyone his cousin was the white Power Ranger to try and stop it happening.

Worked for a couple weeks, they'd all crowd round, ask questions, thought he was cool and then he got sloppy, stories got silly, didn't add up, then one lunchtime he got the beating of his life.

So, I mean, yeah, it happens.

Tim What does that mean? Why are you telling me that?

Marcus Just, sometimes people make things up, but, like, for the right reason.

Tim Yeah, well, this ain't a lie.

Marcus Nah, I know, but you can see why people –

Tim – It's not a lie!

Alright?

They both stare at the photograph for a moment.

Marcus . . . Bet it does your head in, how bad that is.

Tim It's the only one, so . . .

They don't wanna believe it, that it came here and I saw it and they didn't.

Could've let it go, would've made my life easier, but I saw it.

And it's a bit grainy and blurry cos it was a crappy old camera, but I took it.

He came here and I took it.

And I'll prove it.

Marcus And that's your life's work, then, yeah?

You gonna track down Firewing?

Tim No.

You are.

Scene Four

The Hide.

It's now dark outside, very late into the night.

Tim *looks through the lens of the camera to the outside, very occasionally taking a photograph.*

Marcus *stands and stares at the projection of Firewing.*

Tim *checks his watch and looks through the lens again.*

Marcus *looks over at* **Tim**, *gets out his phone and exits.*

Scene Five

The Hide.

It's now sunrise. The sky is waking up; a dark orange which fades into a clear, crisp light blue as the scene progresses.

It's completely still and silent outside.

Firewing is still projected onto the wall.

Tim *is in the toilet.*

Marcus *is checking his phone.*

A weak toilet flush.

Tim *enters.*

Tim Handles piss.

Marcus Right. Great.

Tim Like a dream, it handles piss.

Gotta get a plumber in, never turn up though, do they?

Marcus (*distracted*) Yeah.

Yeah, I know what you mean, mate.

Tim Be nice, be a nice luxury to take a dump without worrying I'll be wading through it later.

Marcus Sounds like luxury.

Tim Won't get much signal in here.

Marcus Just messaging Mum. She's . . . not replying.

Sure she's fine.

Tim *sits at his camera and looks through the lens.*

Silence for a moment.

Marcus This Firewing, then.

Tim Yeah?

Marcus It's rare?

Tim Only time anyone's seen it outside of Siberia.

Marcus Weird, innit?

Tim No.

That's the thing with rare birds.

They're rare.

Marcus And it's never been back?

Tim No, but it will. I know it'll come back.

Marcus Any leads on it?

Tim Got some ideas.

Marcus Yeah?

Tim Taking the piss?

Marcus Nah, sounds, like . . .

Does it, what, does it go home for winter or?

Tim Yeah, for Christmas, see the family.

Marcus In a little scarf, probably. Woolly hat.

Sounds a right laugh, right little character.

Tim Might make a few bob if you find it, but it's not about money, or showing off, it's not about all that, not what matters.

Get that, don't you?

Marcus Yeah.

Marcus *looks up at Firewing.*

Yeah, I get it.

Beat.

Tim *sits at the camera, adjusts it and gets comfortable.*

Beat.

Tim You like travelling about?

Marcus I dunno, yeah.

Not been anywhere too great really.

Tim Get to see some of the world, doing this. Only some of it, mind you, unless you're minted.

Marcus You been all over, then?

Tim Only a few times abroad.

Marcus Yeah, don't matter to me, best bit's coming home anyway, ain't it?

Tim Marcus.

Marcus What?

Tim Don't say that. Dull people say that. Dull people who never leave the house.

Marcus Nah, I do. I do want to, I just –

Tim – See the world outside of South Bridge.

Marcus Huh. Yeah.

Tim You born there?

Marcus Whole family were. But Mum hates it now. They slung all her mates miles away, all the big families she grew up with are gone, and the flats that are still there, they're leaving them to rot.

Wanna get my shit together, put a deposit down on somewhere nice before they kick us out too.

She'd love it here actually, Mum.

Could paint something, knock up something proper with that view.

Tim She any good?

Marcus Yeah.

She painted every weekend. Used to go down the shops and she'd let me pick all the colours, you know, so I'd feel involved. Then she'd come home, stick the radio on and paint, for hours.

And they're better, hers, than most of the dear ones in them posh galleries in town.

Sometimes I imagine walking right in the front door, bang, *'Here's a painting my mum's done, wanna sell it?'*

Wouldn't get a sniff.

Tim If you wanna be heard you gotta go and do something about it.

Marcus She doesn't really, well, doesn't do it much anymore, doesn't really go out, outside the flat or, like, doesn't always get out of bed some days. But.

Beat.

What about your parents, were they, like –

Tim – Were they what?

Marcus Creative?

Tim You're full of questions, ain't you?

Beat.

Marcus *goes to the cubby, checks his phone.*

Tim I'm sure she's alright.

Marcus Yeah.

Yeah, cheers.

Tim *takes a moment.*

Tim . . . My old man, he was . . .

Took care of us, the family, when I was born but . . .

Spent most days avoiding him when I was younger.

Friends stopped coming round so I was out a lot, taking shitty pictures on a shitty little camera.

And I got the hang of it.

So I owe him all this. In a weird sort of way.

Silence for a moment.

. . . It's really important, and I mean *really* important that you never *ever* touch the actual lens, okay?

Marcus *walks into the room.*

Tim You've gotta be serious, Marcus. From now.

Marcus *nods, getting excited.*

Tim There's only one camera. So you have to be careful with it.

Marcus Yeah. Course.

Tim They'll all say you need three or four, in case one jams or if you've got a load of spare cash that wants burning, but it's not the end of the world, is it? I want to capture what's happening and if I can't do it because I'm too slow or there's a problem with the camera, then, well, that's what happened ain't it?

Marcus Yeah. God. Yeah. That's sort of, quite deep.

Tim Don't be daft.

Marcus Right.

Tim When your great, new, flashy camera jams, you work something out, or you don't get the shot. Instinct.

Marcus Bada bing bada boom.

Tim What?

Marcus What about the lens?

Tim Four or five of those but don't get reliant on all the features, they're trying to rob you of your instincts, you have to fight to keep hold of them.

It's who's taking the photograph that matters, not what's taking it.

Tim *gestures for* **Marcus** *to come and stand by the camera.*

Tim Get comfortable.

This is the grip.

Marcus The grip, right, and that's for . . . for gripping, yeah?

Tim Fucking hell. Arse from elbow. Move.

Look. Like this.

You need to be gentle with it, loose, relax.

But take it serious.

Okay?

Marcus Mate, if this was my kit, I'd guard it like a Rottweiler.

I get it.

Tim *stands aside and lets* **Marcus** *sit on the chair and get comfortable in front of the camera.*

Marcus *gently grips the camera for the first time. He is delicate with it.*

Tim *slowly backs away.*

Tim Expecting a family of geese soon. They come round here early.

Camera shy, and they're smart. They'll have no trouble outsmarting you.

They don't like a racket, you'll need to be silent. They'll be right up here, by the window, so breathe through your nose, and very slowly.

You've got one chance at this, they don't hang about, so only take it when you're ready, no do-overs.

Marcus Right.

Tim Be a good start and you can go from there.

Leave the settings for now.

Need to be, just . . .

Marcus *looks through the lens.*

Marcus This okay?

Tim Don't normally get to this point, you know? Taking actual photographs.

And, I was thinking, after this weekend, if you still want to, I can –

Beat.

Tim *watches* **Marcus** *for a moment.*

Marcus Nothing yet. They definitely coming, yeah?

Tim They do a big loop of the lake. Go and see if they're on their way round.

Marcus Yeah. Okay.

Marcus *stands and walks towards the door.*

Marcus . . . It's my dad.

He, er . . .

It's him in prison, not a mate from school.

Marcus *composes himself.*

Sorry. Shouldn't have lied, I just . . .

Tim Oh, I . . .

Marcus He got caught up in some stuff.

That's when it all, with Mum, it just, everything went a bit, downhill.

Tim But, the . . .

Fish eagle?

Marcus On the seafront, that was the last time I saw him.

Tim Oh.

So your old man was there when you took –

Marcus – Can we not?

Sorry.

Sorry, it's just . . . well, that's how I remember it.

And it's, like, we've all got stories to tell, ain't we? And they don't always matter, do they, the exact details?

Tim *nods.* **Marcus** *exits.*

Tim *goes to re-arrange the camera, thinks better of it.*

He stands back, shuts his eyes and takes some deep breaths; gives up control.

Marcus*'s phone, sat in the cubby hole, lights up; it's ringing but on silent.* **Tim** *notices but ignores it.*

Marcus*'s phone lights up again.*

Tim *walks over to the phone and picks it up.*

Tim Hell –

Before he can talk, someone speaks down the phone to him. He's in shock at what he's hearing.

After a moment, he hangs up.

Marcus *walks round the side of the hide, stands still outside, taking in the view of the lake.*

Tim *watches* **Marcus** *through the window.*

Marcus *enters.*

Marcus Can't see them yet.

Be here soon hopefully, yeah?

Beat.

Was just thinking, about this Firewing thing.

Probably could do with getting out a bit more, reconnecting with the world and all that, so, yeah, I think I could help.

If you still want me to.

Those pictures, your photos were, you know, I mean, like, really really good.

Like, I'd love to be able to show them to people, to my mum, put them up on the telly and be like, '*Yeah, I took those*'.

And all that stuff about, you know, creating atmosphere and better photos and stuff, all about the angles and getting me to lie down proper still on the edge of a lake for twelve straight hours just to get a glimpse of a duck's arse, or whatever.

Beat.

Or whatever.

But yeah.

Yeah, I

I'd like to, to, to help or whatever.

Beat.

Shall we get set up for these geese, then?

Reckon we can get a good one from here.

Tim?

Tim Must have been difficult.

Marcus What?

Tim Not having your old man around.

Marcus Oh, um, yeah, a little bit.

Tim Yeah?

Marcus We were alright. Got on with it.

Tim Yeah?

Marcus Yeah.

Tim Why's he locked up, then?

Marcus Oh, just, well,

I don't really –

Tim – He a thief?

Marcus No.

Tim What, worse?

Marcus You alright, mate?

Tim He must be dodgy though, really dodgy?

Marcus Well no, it's just, he –

Tim – Sounds like a wrong 'un to me.

Marcus Mate.

Tim Sounds like a wrong 'un, left his family to it.

Marcus Fuck off.

Tim I know them, that kind of man.

Marcus You don't.

Tim What they're like.

Marcus You don't.

Tim How they mess you up. In here.

End up just like them, don't we?

Tells you how he's changed, how things'll get better, blah blah, but we know –

Marcus – Never even visited him!

Beat.

Alright? I've never . . .

Got to the waiting room, years ago, when I was younger, but I couldn't. They sat me and Mum in these uncomfortable like worn out chairs and I couldn't breathe properly so we had to leave.

Okay?

Every day I . . . and then it just snowballs and before you know it, it's been years.

And you just . . .

Beat.

He's good. Not a wrong 'un. Not at all.

He's, like, he's a good man.

He just did something really bad.

Alright?

Awkward silence for a moment.

Shall we get set up?

Don't wanna miss them.

Tim Heard from your mum?

Marcus Huh?

Tim Get through to her?

Marcus Oh, nah, I'll try again in a bit.

Tim Your phone rang.

Marcus Did it?

Marcus *checks his pockets. Empty.*

He goes to the cubby hole and picks up his phone.

Tim Missed call.

Marcus Shit. Okay.

Tim Rang again, thought it was your Mum.

Marcus Is she okay?

They stare at each other for a moment.

Tim Wasn't her though.

Marcus What?

Tim Wasn't her calling, was it?

Marcus What? I don't –

Tim – It was Jay.

He's sorted it, money's ready,

so you can grab the camera and leave.

A moment.

Marcus . . . Nah, mate, it's . . . it's –

Tim – Did you take the photograph?

Marcus A joke, it's a joke, it's –

Tim – The fish eagle. Did you take that? Did *you* take it?

Tim *looks across at the camera, heartbroken.*

Marcus Mate, this isn't . . .

You can't just, like –

Tim *points at* **Marcus**.

Tim – Don't.

Just fucking don't.

Marcus Story's true, I swear. But . . . I . . . that isn't my picture.

Took one, swear I did. Only had a cheap kid's camera, alright, yeah, there wasn't a lens or anything, that was a lie. Don't think I know where the picture is, if I even kept it, but the story's true. I swear.

Tim The fish eagle photograph, Marcus.

Marcus . . . AI.

It's AI.

Tim *takes a large carrier case from under the sofa.*

Marcus But it's exactly the same, exactly like I remember it.

Tim *places the case on the desk next to the camera and begins to pack it away.*

Marcus But now, I swear, I wanna take photos, proper photos, like you.

Tim *Graphs!* Photo*graphs!*

Tim *continues packing away the camera.*

Marcus Tim?

Tim . . .

So, what, you're just gonna . . . that's it, yeah?

Everything you said, what, we're just forgetting all that?

Did you think you were saving me? Is that what you think you're doing? What? Kids like me, people like *us?*

Waiting for me to mess everything up, so you can say you've tried, lie to yourself, that you've done something, that you are something, cos we're not, are we?

Tim *stops, sits, completely defeated.*

Marcus But at least I

at least

least I know that, least I accept that.

Cos we're all down there, mate, wasting away, you've just got good at pretending you're not.

Beat.

Marcus You're, you're, grooming, that's it, ain't it?

Tim Leave, Marcus.

Marcus Grooming me to help with your work, then drop me soon as you feel like it.

Page seventeen.

What's on page seventeen, Tim?

Aims. Your aims, what about that?

Tim Leave.

Marcus Yeah, what was it, *'Provide opportunities for young people from underprivileged backgrounds'*, was that it? Is that what I am, Tim? Here for charity cos of where I'm from, where *we're* from?

Why don't you read me your aims?

Why don't you read me it?

Cos you can't, can you?

Can't read. Or write.

Beat.

Tim What?

Marcus Don't read the manual, cos you can't. It's obvious, using pictures to communicate –

Tim – Shut up –

Marcus – Cos you can't, not like normal people, can you?

Tim You saw me read the note from your school, you fuckwit.

Marcus Yeah . . . well . . .

Marcus *grabs the manual from the table and holds it in front of* **Tim**.

Tim Marcus –

Marcus – Didn't write this, did you?

What does it say? This bit, what does it say?

Tim?

Marcus *sticks the manual in* **Tim**'*s face.*

Marcus Read it.

Tim Stop.

Tim *snatches it out of his hands.*

Marcus Chasing after a stupid fucking bird? I'm not wasting my life doing that.

Tim *stands, grabs his camera and carelessly, aggressively stuffs it into* **Marcus**'*s hands.*

Tim Take it, just take it.

And fuck off.

What you came for, ain't it?

They stand across from each other for a moment.

Ain't it, Marcus?

Marcus . . . Alright, yeah, I was gonna take it, but it wasn't even my idea, alright? Jay saw the ad and he said if I –

Tim – Can't use it, just sell it, whatever.

Marcus Don't want it now.

Tim Did you hear?

Marcus Changed my mind.

Tim Whatever, Marcus, just take it.

Marcus I tried to call him last night, to cancel it, I messaged him.

Tim Course you did.

Marcus I did. Read my messages.

Tim Take it, and the lenses.

Marcus I told him no.

Tim I can't use it, Marcus. Might as well make some money. That's what you want.

Marcus No, I don't, I . . .

I wanna learn, all this.

Tim Take it.

Marcus I've gotta move Mum out of that flat, I have to, so I . . . I was gonna sell it, but I don't want it anymore.

I wanna learn. With you. Then I can –

Tim – Losing my eyesight.

Beat.

I'm not illiterate.

Couple of months at most, they said.

Getting worse and not gonna improve, so I . . .

Useless to me.

Do what you want with it.

I'm done.

Tim *sits on the sofa.*

After a moment, **Marcus**, *cradling the camera, sits next to him.*

Marcus Can't they, I mean, surely they can –

Tim – They've tried, a few times.

Detached retinas, nothing I can do now.

I'm done.

They sit in silence for a few moments.

Leave, Marcus.

Don't come back here.

Scene Six

The Hide, on the edge of Dawn Lake.

Years ago.

Tim *is nineteen.*

The hut is in disrepair.

Sunlight shines through holes in the ceiling and the walls are beginning to rot. Smatterings of moss spread across the floor and the wooden desk is beginning to crumble. There is only one window; dirty and covered in cobwebs.

One chair sits in front of the desk; no table, no sofa, no fridge, no radio.

The cubby hole is full to the brim of rubbish and debris; old furniture, boxes stacked upon boxes.

The toilet door is at an angle.

Occasional and slight sounds of nature.

Tim, *now nineteen, enters pushing his bike and carrying a large holdall on his back. He wipes his feet at the door.*

Tim's Dad, *late fifties, enters behind him and walks straight through into the Hide, eating a pastry.*

He has crumbs all down his top and mutters as he wipes them off.

Tim's Dad Worrying yourself with wiping your shoes in here?

Wouldn't bother, lad.

Had me waiting out there like a lemon. Thought you'd be here nice and early.

Tim Didn't know you were coming, Dad.

Tim's Dad Tissues, Tim?

Tim What?

Tim's Dad Tissues, boy, mess all down my chops and my shirt, look.

Tim Oh. Yeah.

Tim *opens the toilet door, nearly taking it off its hinges.* **Tim's Dad** *laughs.*

Tim *pulls out some toilet roll and passes it to his dad.*

Tim's Dad Cheers. Always happens. Mucky pup.

Mucky bastard.

Eh? Tim?

Tim Said nothing, Dad.

Tim's Dad Right. No. Just saying, right mucky bastard, I am.

Don't rush to say otherwise.

Tim *forces a laugh.*

They stand in awkward silence for a moment.

Tim's Dad You should have one.

Tim I'm alright.

Tim's Dad Got them, as a little treat.

Tim *cleans the desk with a wet cloth as* **Tim's Dad** *speaks.*

Tim's Dad Remember Bill? Bill Carrick, lived round the back.

Remember, Tim?

Tim Sort of.

Tim's Dad Saw him yesterday, nipped into The Cricketers for a swift half, y'know, and he's telling me his lad Mark's took up a hobby.

Tim Yeah?

Tim's Dad Started collecting records.

Bill said he spends whole days up in his room sometimes, sorting through them, y'know, put them all in alphabetical order, making sure they're all in a neat little row.

Just reminded me of you, that's all.

Thought I should come say hello y'know?

Beat.

Tim . . .

Tim Mum tell you I was here?

Tim's Dad She did, yeah.

How is she?

Tim *walks to the toilet and wrings out his cloth.*

Tim's Dad Never even knew you'd like all this outdoor stuff. Should come fishing with your old man one day, down the river.

Beat.

Bit of a find, this, innit? How'd you swing it?

Tim Teacher's. He left, said I can have it.

Tim *continues cleaning.*

Tim's Dad *walks around, closely examining the walls and floor.*

Tim's Dad Course, Mark's raking in a boatload in his proper job.

Accounts, numbers, all that shit, I don't get it.

But his records, just does that on the side, y'know, in his spare time. It's a hobby, and that's how it's treated.

Tim *slowly, methodically pulls his camera from the holdall and sets it up on the desk, in front of the window, as they speak.*

The camera isn't the best, but it's still impressive, and **Tim** *takes great care with it.*

Tim's Dad Just made me think how long it's been, it's . . .

Don't tell me . . .

Thought, well, you've got your hobby and I wanted to check how everything's going cos, well, life's short, y'know, Tim?

Beat.

Tim's Dad Hear about Kenny?

Tim Kenny?

Tim's Dad Yeah, you remember Kenny.

Tim Rings a bell.

Tim's Dad My cousin. We grew up together, used to bring him round the house when you was only little.

Tim Right.

Tim's Dad You remember?

Tim No.

Tim's Dad Used to play army every lunchtime at school. He was the British and I was always the enemy, y'know, Germany, Japan, whatever. Just me and him.

He died, the other day.

Cancer.

Buried him Friday.

Right fucker.

The cancer, not Kenny.

Coming for us all, y'know? D'ya feel like that sometimes?

Tim?

Tim Came here to cheer me up then, Dad?

Try not to think about it.

Tim's Dad Probably best.

But, y'know, life's short and it needs . . .

Well, hobbies and everything, make sure they're there, obviously, if you want them, but they can get in the way of . . . life, real life.

Tim Dad . . .

Tim's Dad This is valuable advice, Tim. Won't get this from anyone else.

Tim Honestly, for a minute I thought you'd say hobbies are important.

Tim's Dad I was. I did.

Tim That you're happy for me.

Tim's Dad I am.

But you need something that makes you money too, lad, not just something that . . .

You've gotta eat, settle down, family, all that stuff.

Take it from me.

Has a missus and all, does Mark, any news on that front?

Tim Dad. Please.

Tim's Dad *stands behind* **Tim** *and watches him put the camera together.*

Tim's Dad I've . . . er . . .

Tim's Dad *opens his bag and pulls out a small cardboard box. He holds it out in his hand.*

Got you something.

Tim *delicately finishes setting up the camera.*

Tim's Dad Tim.

Tim Just a minute.

Tim's Dad It's not . . . well, I'm not blessed with a heavy wallet, am I, but I found this, thought you'd want it.

Tim *turns and for an awkward moment they look at each other.*

Tim *takes and opens the box.*

Tim's Dad You remember?

Remember that, Tim?

Your first one, weren't it?

Tim *pulls an old, cheap, dirty and well-used camera from the box.*

He stares down at it.

Tim's Dad You remember? When I got it you?

Tim Yeah.

Yeah, thanks.

Thank you . . .

Tim's Dad Going through all my old stuff and I saw –

Tim – Six-and-a-half years, Dad.

Tim *stares down at the camera in his hands as he speaks, avoiding eye contact.*

Tim's Dad What?

. . . No . . . Nah . . . Can't be.

Tim Coming up to seven.

Tim's Dad Bloody hell. Never been that long, has it? Fuck me, it flies, don't it? Gets away from you.

Tim's Dad *moves the chair away from the desk and takes a seat.*

Tim *stands still, staring down at the camera.*

Tim's Dad Seven years . . . Madness, that.

Come and have breakfast with your dad.

Tim Don't eat it.

Tim's Dad What? Why?

An awkward silence.

Tim *walks over to the desk, puts the old camera in his pocket and cleans the round window.*

Tim's Dad *wanders around the cabin again, picking at a bit of rotten wall.*

Tim's Dad Place is really . . .

Tim Can you not do that?

Tim's Dad You'll suffocate in here. This rot, damp, bad for your chest.

Needs a revamp, real sorting out.

Tim I'm gonna do it.

Tim's Dad Ha, what?

Tim Take some time, but it's mine so I'll work it out.

Tim's Dad You won't be able to do it.

Tim Been saving too.

Tim's Dad Yeah?

Tim . . . Yeah.

Tim's Dad No wonder they let you have it, probably a load off their mind, dumping it on you.

Oh, well.

Tim's Dad *pulls a bell off the handlebars of the bicycle in the cubby hole and drops it on the floor.*

Tim's Dad One man's junk, and all that.

Tim *walks over and picks up the bell, attaches it back to the bicycle.*

So, this then . . .

Tim *gets between his dad and his camera.*

Tim's Dad Worth a few bob, no?

Tim Leave that, Dad, I'm serious.

Tim's Dad Don't look like a donation, reckon it's a good bit of kit, this.

Tim Not a donation. I saved up for it. Been working every night, pulling weeds, washing cars.

Working hard, Dad.

Tim's Dad Really?

Tim Really.

So don't touch it.

Really.

Tim's Dad Always guessed, well, hoped really, that you'd finish college, get your trade, do well for yourself, get settled, find a nice woman, you know.

Never thought you'd bury yourself away in a place like this, not in a million years.

Tim I like it in here. I'm happy.

Tim's Dad You're a coward. Hiding from all the people who love you, helped you, raised you.

D'ya know what's happened to all your old friends? Cal, Simon, Jake?

Saw Jake yesterday, d'ya know what he's up to these days, while you're hiding away out here washing cobwebs? Do you?

Fuck all, Tim. Can't find a job to save his life, no one'll have him.

And just cos you've scraped together a bit of cash scrubbing cars and some nonce gave you their old shed, that makes you better than them? Cos they don't hear from you, he told me, none of them do.

Tim (*mumbles*) Weren't friends.

Tim's Dad What?

Tim Weren't my friends, were they?

Tim's Dad Course they were.

Tim Too scared to come in our house after school in case you were in, you mad case!

Tim's Dad Tim.

Tim Didn't want nothing to do with me after that, did they? Like you.

Tim's Dad You can come back, or stay here, but you'll end up alone, in this place, empty. You know that and I know that. Then you can't help anyone, can you? Ungrateful little sod.

Need to look after yourself. Don't even eat . . .

Tim's Dad *storms across the room towards his bag.*

He pulls out a pastry and walks straight at **Tim**.

He grabs the back of **Tim**'*s head and tries to force the pastry into his mouth.*

Tim *splutters the food out, pushes his dad back hard.*

Tim Get

Off!

Dad!

Please!

Tim's Dad I come here, to see you, and you're a mess. It's embarrassing, Tim.

Tim You can't do this anymore. I'm not a child. You'd know that if you'd . . .

Tim *looks right at his dad.*

Tim Six-and-a-half *years.*

Tim's Dad Can't just sit and have breakfast with your dad?

You make me do this, I come to make sure you're alright, bring you something nice and you throw it back at me, upset me. Can't take care of yourself, can you?

Tim *walks to the cubby hole and opens the end of one of the bicycle handlebars. From a hidden compartment he pulls out a small handful of notes.*

Tim Know why you're here, I'm not stupid.

He shoves the money into his dad's hand and walks to the door.

Tim's Dad Tim, I was –

Tim – Just know that's all I have so don't bother coming back here, I ain't got anything left for you take, neither does Mum. Do what you want, you always have done.

But if you touch that.

Tim *points at his camera.*

I'll never forgive that.

Tim *exits and walks round the front of the Hide and stands at the foot of the lake.*

Tim's Dad *looks down at the cash.*

Tim *stands, head tilted to the sky, and takes big, deep breaths to calm himself.*

Tim's Dad *pockets half the cash, leaves the other half next to the camera and exits.*

Tim *hears something from behind the Hide and stands to look but can't see over it. He tracks the noise round the front of the Hide and suddenly spots something in the sky.*

He considers running back inside for a split second, but realising he won't make it in time, he searches his pockets and pulls out the old camera.

He takes a rushed photograph and tries to take another but the camera jams.

He looks up and watches Firewing fly off into the distance.

He sits at the foot of the lake.

Scene Seven

The photograph of Firewing fades in.

Then fades back out.

The Hide, on the edge of Dawn Lake.

Present day again.

The old sofa and chair remain, everything else has gone.

The cubby hole is empty except for a suitcase.

The toilet door is fixed.

Clattering and bashing noises from inside the toilet.

Tim *enters, looking frail and old.*

Wearing sunglasses, a battered camouflaged coat and thick steel toe boots, he waves a cane in front of him as he walks through the cabin.

The noises from the toilet stop.

Tim Oi!

Hello?

The noises start again.

Tim *thumps the toilet door as hard as he can.*

The noise stops.

Oi!

Marcus *steps out into the cabin.*

Tim What you doing? Get out, nothing valuable in here.

Marcus . . . Tim?

Tim *finds his way to the sofa and sits.*

Marcus Tim, I . . .

It's Marcus.

Beat.

Marcus Good to see you.

Beat.

Marcus How are you?

Tim Told you not to come back.

Awkward silence for a moment.

Marcus I've just been, you know, sorting things. Fixing it up a bit.

Tim Just you?

Marcus Just me.

Tim *nods, deep in thought.*

Tim Dennis called, from the shop, said someone's been in here, messing around.

Marcus Not messing around.

Tim Was worried. Doesn't want kids running riot. He kept calling so I said I'd come and clear everything out, get him off my back.

Marcus Been coming the last few weeks. Didn't know if . . . Didn't seem right, just sat here empty.

Beat.

Marcus Heard about the award. Congrats.

Tim They just want me in a room so they can look at me.

Marcus Celebrating your work, nah?

Tim Same bastards who said I lied about Firewing.

Marcus So, you're not going?

Tim Nah.

Could send a decoy.

Or lock them all in and let loose a plague of locusts.

Where can I get locusts?

Marcus *wheels the suitcase out from the cubby hole.*

Tim *looks up at the wall where his photographs were once projected.*

Marcus *notices him.*

Marcus Can you remember them? Your pict . . . your photographs?

Tim They told me, when they knew my sight wasn't gonna get better, they said I should spend time looking at things I like, things that make me happy, spend as much time as I can looking at them, to keep them in my head when everything goes to black.

Couldn't bring myself to do it, not properly.

So I can remember a few of them.

Least, I hope I'm remembering them right.

Marcus They're quality, mate. Took the projector and showed Mum, she loved them.

Tim How is she?

Marcus Yeah, she's alright. Stays indoors a lot still, but.

Yeah. Started painting again.

Only a little bit, but, small steps and all that.

Still in the same place, but I'm working on it, always working on that.

And I'm working on this place too, just getting it up to scratch, you know?

Tim Right.

Marcus Nah, I am. Can't just let it rot.

Tim Did you sell it?

Marcus It'll brush up alright, this place.

Tim Marcus, did you sell the camera?

Marcus No.

I didn't, no.

Tim You should sell it.

Marcus Thought I'd just grab it, be gone before anyone could prove it. Jay saw the ad and he knows all about the kit, how much it's worth. He sold all my Dad's stuff when he . . .

He convinced me, said it'd be easy. But when I think about it, it seems a bit, well, you know, thick.

I should have told him to sod off.

Shouldn't have lied, Tim, I shouldn't have. I know that and I'm . . .

Just wanted, like, for Mum, and . . .

But I'll sort it. I'll sort something.

Tim Just sell it.

Marcus Been walking past those posh as shit galleries up the high street every day, back and forth, looking through the window. I'll go in there one day, reckon I could get them to take one of her paintings.

There's this one, it was Dad's favourite, a big landscape of the field behind their first flat. They'll really like that one.

And Banksy sells stuff for millions and millions I think, doesn't he, so . . . yeah.

Tim Marcus.

Marcus And I'm working now, little café.

Tim Marcus.

Marcus Said they might let me in the kitchen on quiet days.

Tim Marcus, sell the camera, then you can put it towards the –

Marcus – Nah.

Still got a massive manual to get through, ain't I?

Tim Always knew you were thick as a plank.

Marcus *grins.*

Marcus And I come out here on the weekends, when I can get them off.

Marcus *cleans.*

Tim You kept the slides?

Marcus Yeah. They were in a box of stuff in the cubby, so I . . .

I can bring them back, I'll –

Tim – No.

Keep them.

Marcus Wanna try and take some like that myself. Get proper good at it.

And Firewing. I dunno, I just, I feel like I really need to see it.

And I want to.

That's why I'm here, right?

Tim . . . You're here cos your application was short.

Drew me to it. Simple.

And lucky for you, I like simple.

It was the last entry you know, got it in just before the deadline. Lazy sod.

Got some absolute essays in a couple of the applications, never gonna read them.

Marcus Could've missed out on some right genius, then, someone a lot smarter than me.

Tim Son, it's an absolute given they'd have been smarter than you.

Marcus *can't help but smile.*

Tim Your postcode. Got excited when I saw that.

Been waiting for someone to apply from there for years.

Couldn't believe my luck, thought you'd be the one to . . .

Fish eagle photograph was alright, but . . . you know . . .

Marcus *cleans.*

Tim A lot quieter here these days.

Really notice that now.

Marcus Yeah.

Still get a lot of, you know, birds and everything. Had this deer walking round last week, think it was lost, it was all panicked, but it ran off.

Silence for a moment.

Booked a visit to see Dad.

And, you know, by the time he's out I'm sure we'll be sorted with a new place and he can come and live with me and Mum there.

He'll like it I think.

We'll have a really big garden I reckon, probably a bungalow so it's easier for Mum, you know? One of them shower rooms and a massive kitchen with an island probably and a big fuck off fridge. And a coffee machine. Big barbecue out the back with like four grills on it.

But somewhere with a proper view, like by a big field with a river or something.

Tim *sits back, takes in the feel of this place he loves.*

Marcus And you should, er, come round.

Some time.

I'll grow some stuff in the garden as well, tomatoes, carrots. Did you know you can grow cauliflower?

Tim Yeah.

Marcus But like, out of the ground, in your own garden if you want to?

Tim Well . . . yeah.

Marcus So I could make us like a whole roast dinner and only have to buy the chicken.

Tim . . . I'll think about it.

Marcus *smiles; he knows he won't.*

Marcus *watches* **Tim** *for a moment.*

Marcus I'm off in a minute, mate.

Only came to see if I could give the bog a seeing to.

Still won't flush.

Silence for a moment.

Tim Son.

Marcus Yeah, mate.

Tim You believe me about Firewing?

Marcus Course.

Tim Give anything to see it again.

Beat.

But I saw it once.

Didn't I.

Tim *sinks down into his chair.*

Marcus *pulls the camera carry case from his suitcase and opens it.*

Marcus *cleans the camera.*

Tim *looks up in the direction where he once saw Firewing.*

Lights fade.

End.

www.ingramcontent.com/pod-product-compliance
Lightning Source LLC
LaVergne TN
LVHW052338100826
845147LV00020B/1109

9781350654747